Big Digger
abc

Margaret Mayo   **Alex Ayliffe**

ORCHARD

Aa

Ambulance

Busy, busy ambulance
rush, rush, **rushing**.
whee-**OW!** whee-**OW!**
Loud siren blaring.

Bulldozer

Bb

Tough bulldozer
push, **push, pushing.**
Over bumpy ground,
scraping and shoving.

Cc

Crane

Very tall crane
hoist,
hoist,
hoisting.
Up go the bricks
to the top of the building.

Digger

Dd

Great big digger
dig, **dig**, *digging.*
Scooping up the earth,
lifting and tipping.

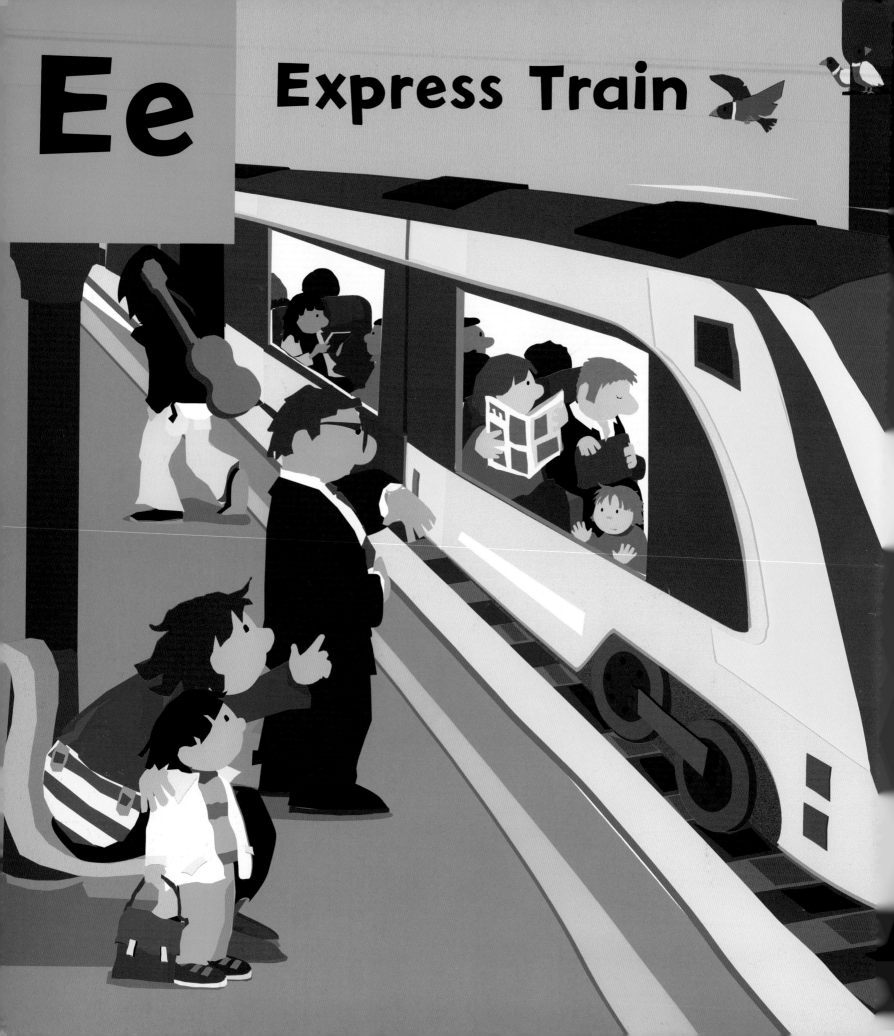

Ee Express Train

Super-fast express train
speed, speed, speeding.
Racing down the tracks – wh**oo-oom!**

At stations stopping.

Ff

Fire Engine

Shiny red fire engine
dash, dash, **dashing.**

Nee-**nar!** Nee-**nar!**

Bright lights flashing.

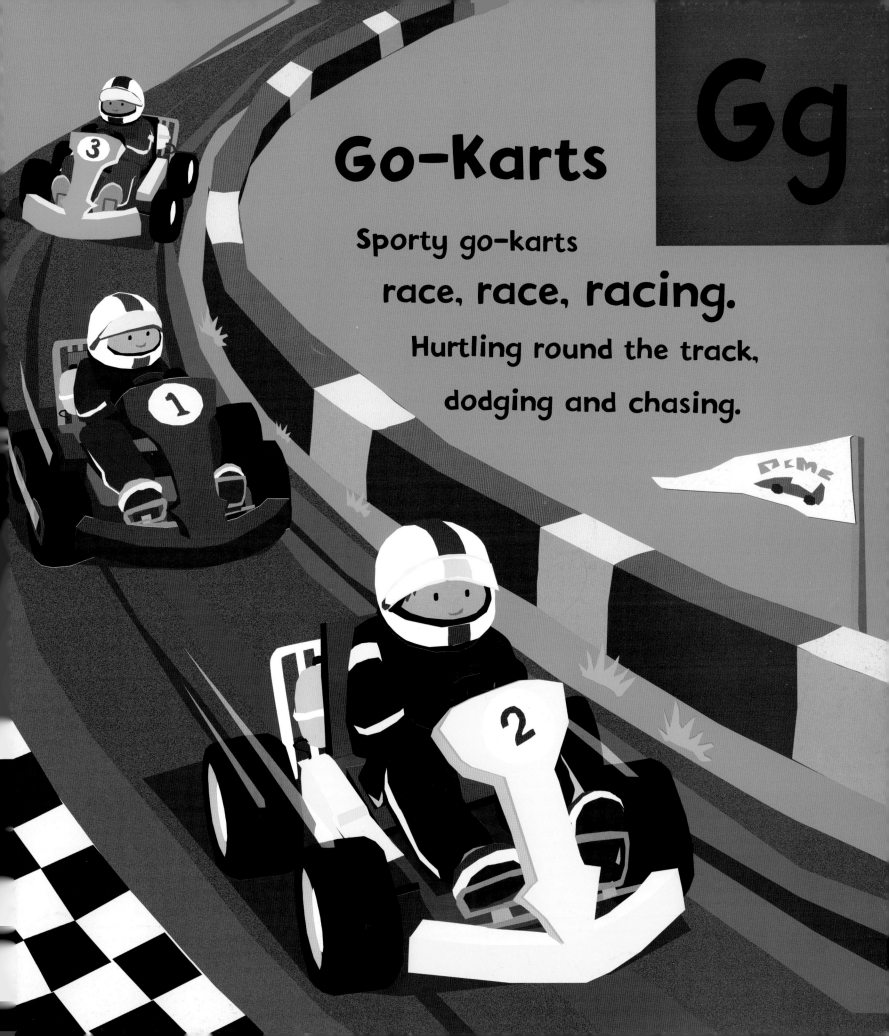

Go-Karts

Gg

Sporty go-karts
race, **race, racing.**
Hurtling round the track,
dodging and chasing.

Hh

Helicopter

Smart yellow helicopter

whirr, whirr, whirring.

Hovering and swaying –

look!

Someone needs rescuing.

Icebreaker

Ii

Powerful icebreaker
crack, crack, cracking.
Ploughing through the ice,
crunching and smashing.

Jj

Jumbo Jet

Enormous jumbo jet
roar, **roar**, **roaring.**
Over fields and buildings,
up . . . **up . . .**

soaring!

Kk

Kayak

Racing river kayak
swoosh, swoosh, swooshing.
Rushing over rapids,
paddle safely guiding.

Lorry

Hardworking lorry
beep, beep, beeping.
Rumbling down the motorway,
heavy loads transporting.

Mm Motorbikes

High-speed motorbike
vroom, **vroom**, **vrooming.**

Swooping . . . swerving . . .

Careful now!

No crashing!

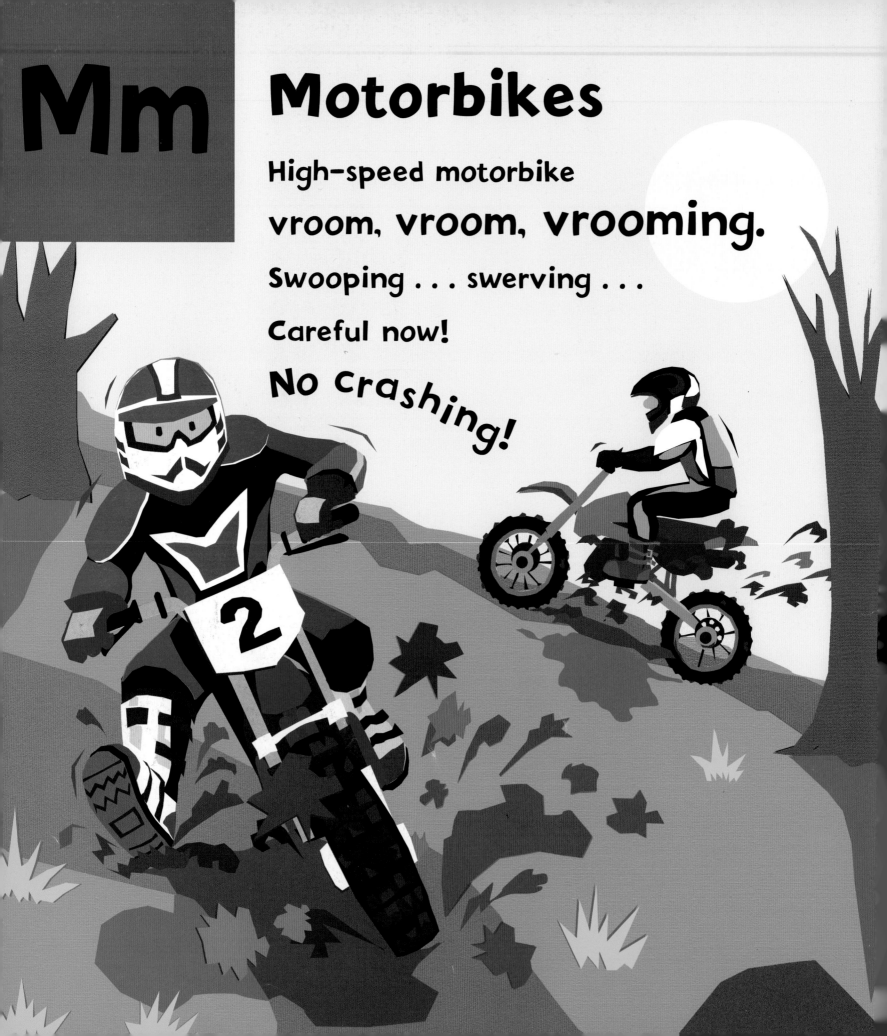

Narrowboat

Nn

Brightly-painted narrowboat
chug, chug, chugging.
Along peaceful waterways
slowly gliding.

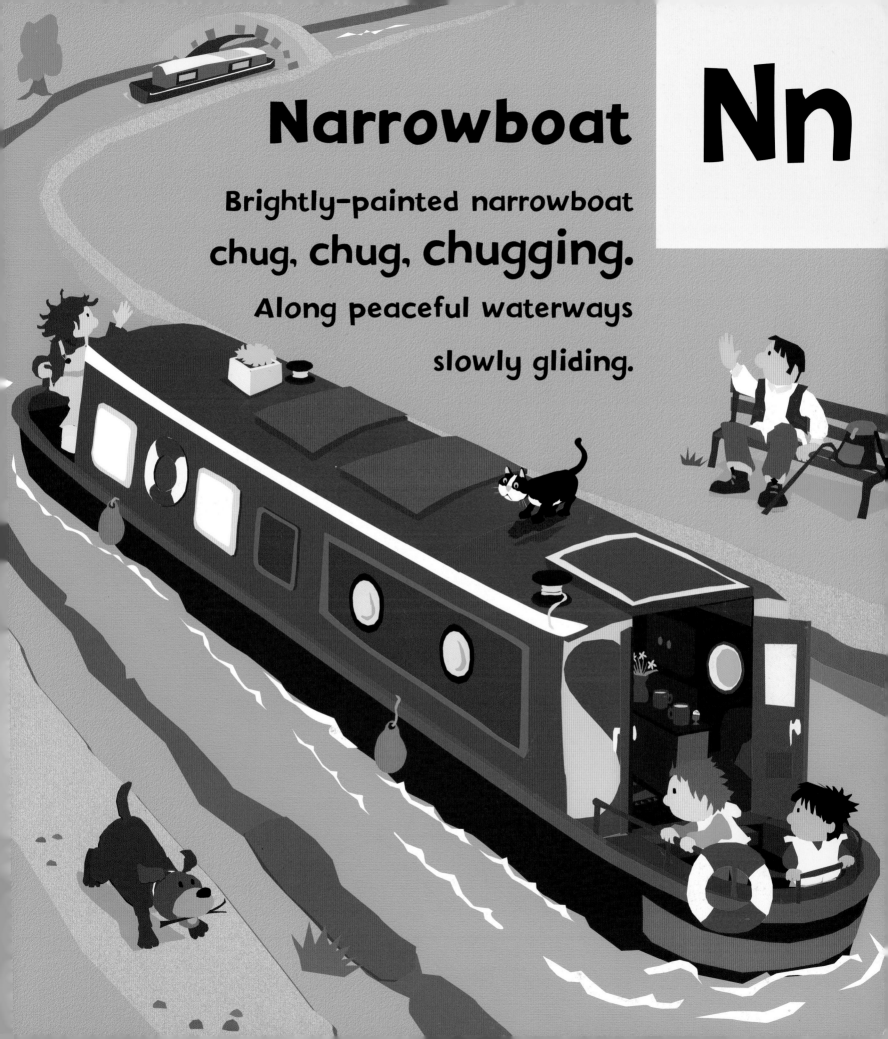

Oo

Ocean Liner

Luxury ocean liner
cruise, cruise, cruising.
Climb aboard for lots of fun
and round-the-world sailing.

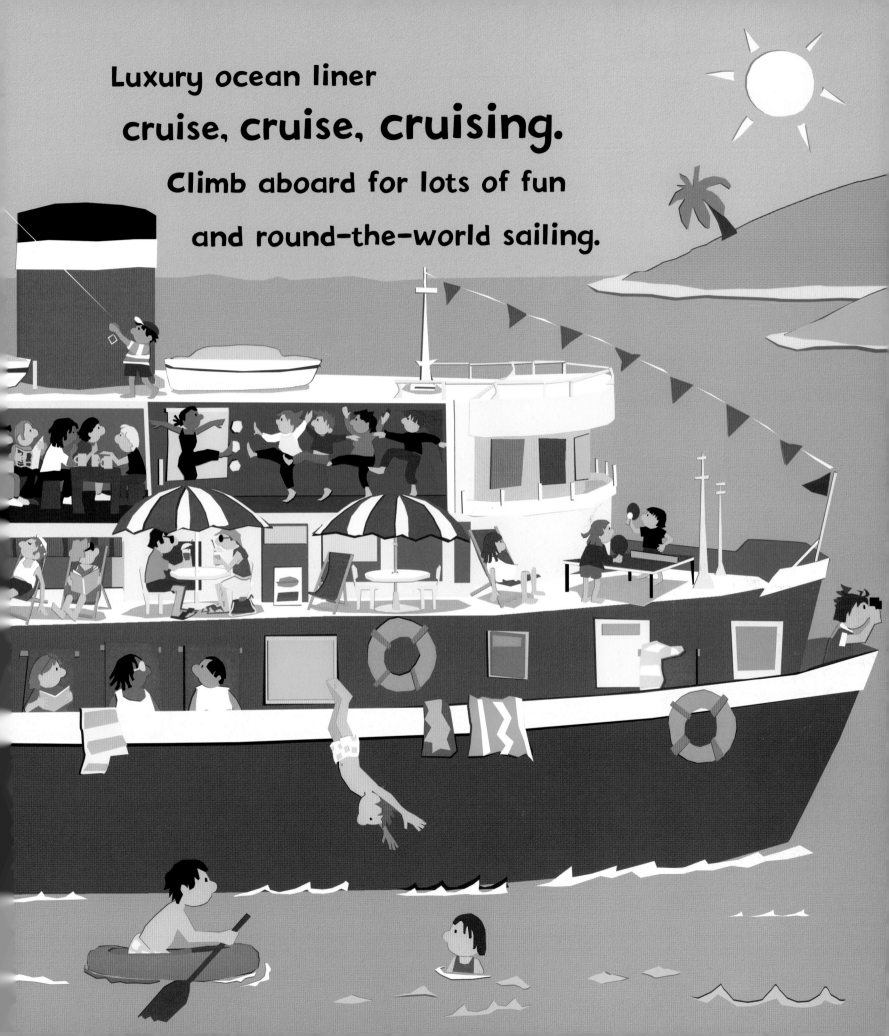

Pp

Police Car

Emergency police car

scream,

scream,

screaming.

Slow down! Make way!

Police overtaking!

Qq

Quad Bike

Sturdy quad bike
bump, bump, bumping.
Along rough paths and up steep hills,
climbing and exploring.

Rubbish Truck

Rr

Noisy rubbish truck
gobble, **gobble, gobbling.**
Crunching messy bin bags,
squeezing and squashing.

Ss

Scooter

Super little scooter
scoot, scoot, scooting.
Strong foot pushing,
and it's off . . . racing!

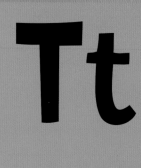

Tt

Tractor

Tough yellow tractor
pull, pull, pulling.
ploughing up the field,
wheels squelch, squelching.

Underwater Robot

Uu

Underwater robot

dive,

dive,

diving.

In the deep, dark sea

lost treasures finding.

Vv

Velodrome Track Bike

Velodrome track bike
whizz, whizz, whizzing.
Pedals turning, wheels whirling,
but – wow! – NO BRAKES
for stopping!

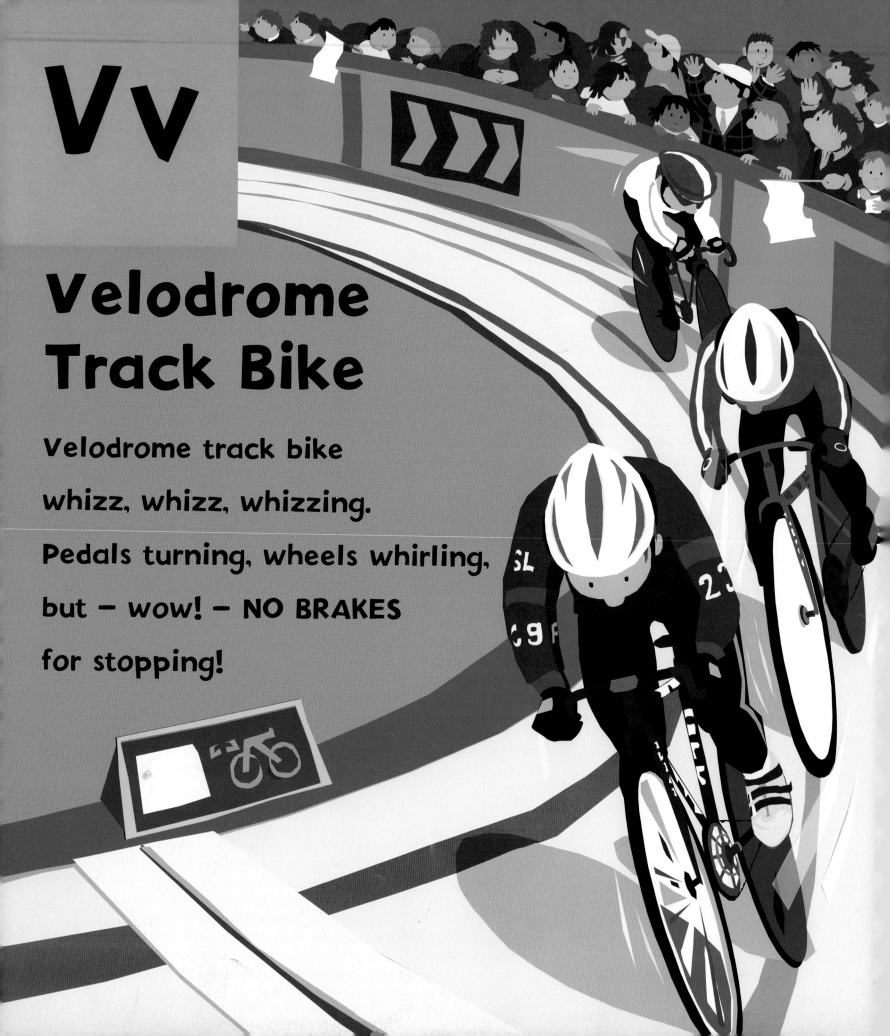

Ww

Wind-Surfing Kite

wind-surfing kite
fly, fly, flying.
Surfer, hold tight . . .
ready for fast water-riding!

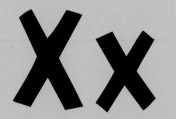

Xx

EXtra Big Wheels

EXtra-big-wheeled monster truck
grrhumm, grrhumm, **grrhumming.**
Fast racing, clever jumping and –
WHAM! – crazy wheel-standing.

Yacht

Yy

Beautiful yacht,
sail, sail, sailing.
Waves lapping, water splashing,
sails flap, flapping.

Zz Zooming Rocket

Mighty, mighty rocket
zoom, zoom, zooming.
5 4 3 2 1 ... and ...
BLAST OFF!

LAUNCHING!

zoooming!